Rough Road

The Government Exists Only in Name in Afghanistan

Wazhma Khalili

*Our mission is to efficiently provide the world's finest, most comprehensive book publishing
service, enabling every author to experience success. To find out how to publish your
book, your way, and have it available worldwide, visit us online at www.trafford.com*

Trafford rev. 10/27/2010

 **Trafford**
PUBLISHING® www.trafford.com

North America & international
toll-free: 1 888 232 4444 (USA & Canada)
phone: 250 383 6864 ♦ fax: 812 355 4082

Books by this author;

Rough Road;
The Government Exists only in name in Afghanistan

The New Edition: The Truth;
A Way Out of the Wilderness:
Muslim-Views during the Election of 2008

The Truth;
A Way Out of the Wilderness:
Muslim-Views during the Election of 2008

ISBN: 1-4392-3236-9
ISBN-13: 9781439232361

BookSurge

Please feel free to voice your opinion and learn more about the author at her website;

www.wazhmathetruth.com

Dedication

I would like to dedicate, my second book, to my precious and lovable parents. To my amazing dad Motasimbilla Khalili, my magnificent mother Alia Khalili and my little love, my precious child, Sarah Khalili Khan. They have all been there for me and supported me throughout my education. Each one of you means the world to me. I love you all from the bottom of my heart.

Thank you

Dean Abed Almala

For being there for me when I needed you, and always providing me with a great leadership. Throughout my time at Strayer University, you have always gone out of your way to support me. You are quite an amazing and astonishing Dean at Strayer University. Thank you once again Dean Almala for everything you have done for me.

Thank you to my very best friend

James Uba

For helping me with making my website, and for helping me with putting my work to file for me. Throughout these twelve years of friendship, you always were there for me when I needed you the most. Thanks once again for your true friendship.

x

Thank you to Al Underwood for editing

my book for me

Al Underwood

Thank you for offering to help me with editing my book for me and supporting me with this book. Thanks for your friendship and for your kindness once again for standing by me to help me to be successful.

Acknowledgment

I would like to take a moment and thank some very special people in my life, my very amazing niece Hannah Nurzay, my lovely nephew Abraham Nurzay, my very special nephew Noah Jaghori, and my very sweet nephew Sherman Stewart III. You all mean the world to me. I love each of you very much.

Sarah and the rest of you all are the apple of my eye.

Peace:

Sending my love and my peace, to my Americans, and Muslims family, and friends who have shown, support and love for my first book. Thank you for the encouragement that you all have given me to write other true stories.

Table of Contents

CHAPTER 5

Forward

In this book, I will scrutinize several main points in Afghanistan public administration and Afghanistan foreign policy of the United States towards Afghanistan. I will show you why I believe the United States should take major action towards Afghanistan to stop this power from further ongoing abuse. Afghanistan is a democratic country but does not operate as such. However, the executive official who dictates supremely abuses his power and authority. In the United States, the public administration legislates both statewide and federally; but when power is, abused, there are checks and balances to stop the corruption, and consequences for these mistakes.

"A politician thinks of the next election - a statesman, of the next generation."

- James Freeman Clarke

Chapter 1

Introduction

I will examine the three main areas in Afghanistan Public Administration. First, public Administration exists only in name in Afghanistan. Second, the United Nations has no power or capability over the Taliban, and third, the Karzai Regime has no power over the Taliban. The Indian subcontinent, Iran, flanks Afghanistan's region and central Asia has lured subjugators throughout history. Its high mountains assist the ethnic groups that reside there to defend their sovereignty.

It is apparent that there was a well-developed culture in Afghanistan in ancient times. Undoubtedly cultures had grown in the north and east before the Persian king Darius I (c.500 B.C.) subjugated this region. Later, Alexander the Great dominated (329–327 B.C.) them on his way to India. This is why Hosseine wants to tell the truth, because just like Alexander the Great, everyone wants to dominate

Afghanistan. As an Afghan woman, I will do everything in my power to help afghan people in Afghanistan to see the freedom, to be able to receive the sunlight and the education that they deserve. Children in Afghanistan cry for a piece of food.

This is not what we call government. If the government cannot provide food, shelter, or schools, we do not consider it as a valid government. The government of Afghanistan does not care about its people enough to provide what they need to survive.

Chapter 2

History of Afghanistan

Afghanistan's first name was Arena and then changed to the name Kharasan Balk, it was the main region for Islam. The main languages Afghans speak are Dari, and Pashto.

Alexander the Great was the very first conqueror that used Afghanistan as the main entrance to enter into India. Islamic subjugation was there in the 7th century, and all Afghan men, women, and even the kids are very possessive of their land, faith, and of their religion and heritage. It is more vital for their freedom than their life.

Most people know Afghans for their faithfulness, and for fighting to protect their country.

Public Administration in Afghanistan

Afghanistan used to have a Parcham regime. Parcham means "flag" according to Frank Clements. He wrote in his book, Conflict in Afghanistan, "faction was the Parcham (meaning "flag"), which was less Pashtun-oriented and recruited students and teachers from the schools of the wealthy and from Kabul University" (Clement, 2003). It is very clear that Parcham is more of the development, educational, bright future for everyone;

but unfortunately, the Taliban did not let it happen.

According to Neamatollah Nojumi, who writes about the rise of Taliban in Afghanistan; "This ideological Confrontation caused the PDPA (Party for Democratic Prosperity) in 1966 to crack into two factions after only 18 months of establishment: Parcham faction under Babrak Karmal; and Khalqis under Noor Mohammad Taraki, Parchamis "criticized the Khalqis for being too openly and outspokenly socialist." (Nojumi, 2002). Afghanistan is a democratic country today. It also has a first amendment.

The Afghan people and current government body do not follow their public administration; and unfortunately after the year 1992, they do not follow any specific role or law in Afghanistan.

According to Kenneth Katzman, who is a Specialist in Middle Eastern Affairs Foreign Affairs, Defense, and Trade Division; "For the first time ever, Afghanistan has a fully elected government", although there were parliamentary elections during the reign of King Zahir Shah (the last were in 1969)." (Katzman, 2006). The year 1992 was when the Taliban invaded Afghanistan.

There will be a very tough, extensive and very exigent road for Afghanistan to find its right pathway towards solidarity, and to have a successfully legitimate government body. Currently they do not have a justifiable government to which they all are looking. There will be little chance for any Afghan to have a voice in their government. The Government manipulates its people by saying, "not to worry, we will listen to you all". However, once the government gets what it wants, then they will turn their back on the people. It is very hard for people to trust their government, because they always say one thing and do another. The Afghanistan government barely keeps its promise to the people.

At this point, they believe that only the international community can rescue them. The Afghanistan government will try to manipulate the system by saying, yes, we are trying to help people and yes, we hear their voices. On the other hand, the government will do the very opposite of what they initially promised they would do. There is a very powerful voice of the Afghan people trying to reach out to the International Community. The voice screams out for the world to come and help the Afghan people to cease this ongoing powder keg of abuse in Afghanistan.

The people hope that one day the international community will come around and help them to end the fighting, and to help them with rebuilding their home. I will scream with them and for them, asking for international help. This is a very important time in Afghanistan. The former president of Afghanistan Dr. Najibullah, was president of Afghanistan in the years 1987-1992. Dr. Najibullah was born in 1947.

Afghanistan was invented by Taliban, and Mujadeen. Dr. Najibullah sought refuge with the United Nations, but was, executed by Taliban in 1992. Taliban kidnapped Dr. Najibullah from the United Nations building (Wikipedia).

Neither the Afghan government nor the United Nations could step in to prevent this atrocity from happening. Even the police did not try to stop this kind of abuse that was happening in Afghanistan.

Governance of Afghanistan

The main reason for my paper is to find
the true and accurate answer for my
question and to help my country to get
out of this ongoing fight: to find peace
in the mind and heart of the people.
Sarah Lister is the Governance and Civil
Society Advisor at the Oslo Governance
Center. Lister explains how poor the
public administration is in Afghanistan.
There is a lack of leadership, according to
Lister. In addition, "Afghanistan measures

up poorly on most of these elements. In particular, strong domestic political leadership is lacking." (Lister, 2006) Afghanistan's goal and agenda has been unworkable and manageability among supporters has become poor.

Understandably, both urbanized and emerging countries maintain that the modification of the public administrative body is tremendously difficult. Corruption drains the money away from federal employees.

According to the World Bank report, in the South Asia region "non-salary budget execution for SY1381", the consequence is that they cannot do their jobs, or they are forced to be dependent on local commanders, including other political elite who can provide funds to repair school windows or provide other non-salary running" (World Bank).

Estimates of how much money the U.S. government channeled to the Afghan rebels over the next decade varies, but most sources put the figure between three and six billion dollars or more. Whatever the exact amount, this was "the largest covert action program since World War II". Much bigger for example, than Washington's intervention in Central of America at the same time, which was received considerably more publicity. After all this money spent in Afghanistan, the Afghans do not see any improvement. That is why Gasper says that Public Administration exists in name only in Afghanistan (Gasper, 2001).

Here, we can all see and feel why the Afghanistan administration is poor. Since the government pays their employees very little, they do not do good work to improve their country's ties, rebuild Afghanistan, and improve education. The employees view their government with indifferent eyes, which is sad. The Afghan government should stand up and ask the international community for help. The government should pay their employees better salaries, and should hear their voice to help their country rebuild and restart. Doing nothing and cheating the public will not improve our country, and it will remain where it is right now. Colonel Vincent M. Dreyer is the United States Army Project Adviser:

He mentions, "The Afghan government's capacity to help its own people by improving public Administration and training government officials and Afghan NGOs to train other Afghans." (Colonel Vincent 16). I agree with this author. First Afghanistan needs to improve its public administration, and then focus on ceasing the ongoing fighting within the country. There is a definite lack of communication in the government, because all that the public administration focuses on, is how to destroy their country and not how to rebuild it. Therefore, we definitely need the international community to help us rebuild.

Chapter 3

The Role of the International Community

Afghanistan is always grateful to get help and assistance from the international community. The international community must be able to assist this country during its time of need and while in a crisis, such help will come from the United Nations and the United States. Similar stories as Hosseni's happen in Afghanistan every day. Afghanistan has definitively not yet stabilized. Recently the international community has been involved in solving these ongoing issues.

The international community's role should be to help the Afghan government to guarantee the protection of the environment, in rebuilding, and in the development of the country.

Agustin Carstens was in office as Deputy Managing Director of the International Monetary Fund from 2003 to 2006. Agustin mentions the very important roles in Afghanistan, and how it plays by the international government, to help rebuild Afghanistan. "The authorities focused initially on crisis management and establishing or rebuilding key economic institutions and providing basic government services".

The authorities of international community governments are focusing on the economy, and how to rebuild Afghanistan, which will hopefully; give new life to the Afghan people. (Agustin, 2004). Greg Sheridan, a foreign newspaper editor, writes in his article, US Strategy In Afghanistan Deserves More Than Lip Service: "This is not remotely to criticise the performance of our magnificent troops on the ground. However, our performance in Afghanistan shows how we have slipped from being a genuinely serious nation militarily, and our apparent inability to engage in serious military activity." Nevertheless, it is decisive in two other ways.

The Afghan defence force must prove that it can, in fact work, that it can battle with the Taliban and perform with regulation. They should be very determined to do this with partnership troops serving as well. Ultimately, the Afghan defence force will need to do it alone.

Josh Rogin, who is in charge of national security and foreign policy, also writes a daily web column. In the past, he worked on foreign policy for Afghanistan, and Iraq. According to Rogin, "The idea of getting our foreign assistance as directly to the people who are going to use it as efficiently as

Possible, is central to the way we're thinking about foreign assistance and development generally".

Lew said, adding that since many of the contracts were up for renewal at the beginning of October, it gave the impression this transfer was more immediate and widespread than it necessarily was" (Rogin October 2009.) As we can see now, the help through the international community has had a big impact in Afghanistan. It has given Afghans hope that one day Afghanistan could get rebuilt, and the warfare will cease. Afghanistan once was very beautiful, with many educated people.

Summary

I believe that Public Administration exists in name only in Afghanistan, based on many reasons that I have given above. As I mentioned earlier, our Public Administration do everything for its own interest and benefit, it is careless about public interests. I also mentioned that the United Nations has no power over Taliban because, Taliban kidnapped the former president of Afghanistan. Neither the Afghan government nor the United Nations had bothered to step in and stop this abuse from happening.

They are careless about what their public or their employees need, as the Afghanistan government pays their employees very low wages. The Afghanistan public administration only focuses on their, own agenda and not on national interests. The innocent people of Afghanistan are very afraid to cry out for help. They believe that if they ask for help, the government of Afghanistan might sentence them to death, or they might even end up losing their family, or their kids might be kidnapped from their home. That is why we should not call it a government. It is sad enough to see how people in other countries go through with their public administrations like in

Afghanistan. Public Administration should wake up and start asking to help them to rebuild our country. The Public Policy in Need of Immediate Change: Foreign Policy of United States toward Afghanistan.

Chapter 4

The foreign policy of the United States should take immediate action towards Afghanistan to stop the abuse of power. In Afghanistan, the executive official who is in power overlooks his power and ability. In the United States, its foreign policy legislates both statewide and federally; but when policies are, mistreated, there are checks and balances to discover and correct fraud, and punish disreputable behavior. At one time, there was a democratic culture in Afghanistan.

The foreign policy of the United States needs to take immediate action towards Afghanistan to prevent those in power from allowing abuse to happen in the future. The tall, gorgeous mountains of Afghanistan contain tribal groups who live there and defend their rule. There are many challenges to change Afghanistan's government.

Literature Review

Afghanistan's original name was Arena, which then changed to Kharasan Balk; this was the first Islamic province. There are two languages Dari, and Pashto, which people speak in Afghanistan today. Alexander the Great was the first one who used Afghanistan to gain access to India. Islamic captors were there in the seventh century, and all Afghan children, women, and men were very proud of their devotion to land, religion and traditions.

People in Afghanistan valued their liberty more than their lives.

Most people know Afghans for their authenticity, and in fighting to protect their country, as long as it takes, and as hard as it may be. Afghans will die for their motherland. I will analyze why public policy needs to be, changed immediately in Afghanistan, with the United States' help. The United States has been proficient at focusing its concentration abroad to protect life and liberty. Currently the main focus of President Obama is on how to completely stop corruption in Afghanistan. Current news has shown that the public administration in Afghanistan needs to change right away. Recently, US Army

Soldiers found one trillion dollars worth of "untapped mineral".

According to Blake Hounshell, he writes that "The United States has discovered nearly $1 trillion in untapped mineral deposits in Afghanistan, far beyond any previously known reserves and enough to fundamentally alter the Afghan economy and perhaps the Afghan war itself, according to senior American government officials." Now with this one trillion dollar potential resource, Afghanistan does not need any more monetary support. The only support the Afghan people need from the US, is advice on how to use the money from these minerals properly.

I believe that President Obama has a tremendously good strategy for Afghanistan; "One of America's growing problems in public policy is that it increasingly confuses concepts with strategy to the point where this is becoming a social disease. In the real world, a strategy must include a clear assessment of what action is necessary and the goal to be achieved; that is an assessment of key options, of cost-benefits and risks.

The selected option must be supported by detailed implementation plans, a detailed description of the actions required and a schedule for taking them, a detailed description of the resources required and how to obtain them, and measures of effectiveness to show whether or not it is successful once implemented." (Cordesman 2008). President Obama has a very clear mission, and a set plan to focus on Al Qaida and Bin Laden, to remove them from Afghanistan and to be an aid for public policy to help turn around the economy in Afghanistan. (Blake, 2010). In addition, we need to find a way to stop drug abuse in Afghanistan.

The United States needs to get involved to help change public policy in Afghanistan, by stopping drug protection and abuse. There are no public policies in Afghanistan, which have addressed this issue seriously. According to Antonio

Maria Costa, "The problem reached historic proportions in 2007 - as UNODC reported, 193,000 hectares of poppy were cultivated, producing a record 8,200 tons of opium. On aggregate, Afghanistan's opium production has reached a frightening new level, twice the amount produced two years ago. No other country - since China in the 19th century - has ever Produced narcotics on such a deadly scale." (Costa 2008).

This is actually one of the biggest reasons for immediate attention from the US. As President Karazi mentioned, these drugs should be, eliminated soon, before they damage more of the country and the Afghan people.

Summary

While I was searching, for materials for my study, what I read really opened my eyes, and I found out what the poor and unknowledgeable Afghan men, women, and kids are going through on a day-to-day basis. Afghans need some immediate attention from the United States right away, so the US can stop the abuse of authority in Afghanistan. This ongoing abuse damages Afghanistan as a country, the people and the children. This is important for every country.

Chapter 5

The Role of
the United States

The Afghan people and Afghan government are constantly thankful for receiving support from the US government. The foreign policy of America has taken an immediate action towards Afghanistan based on these issues: improving the US and Afghanistan partnership, security, and economics.

According to Kenneth Katzman, "In the U.S.-Afghan partnership, U.S. diplomats are adjusting their approach to Afghan President Hamid Karzai, who was weakened by 2009, early 2010 U.S. criticism of his failure to curb corruption and by the extensive fraud in the August 20, 2009, presidential elections." (Katzman June 2010). The author mentioned that the Obama Administration believes the security situation may be weakening, regardless of an ongoing enhanced U.S. military presence during 2006-2008. Assessments have resulted in a resolution to add battle troops, with the intention of generating the circumstances to increase Afghan governance and economic improvement, rather than on following and overpowering rebellion. (Katzman June 2010). According to the US Department of State, Afghanistan has made considerable progress since the Taliban was deposed in 2001.

However, the country still has difficult challenges ahead, including defeating terrorists and radicals, amending for over three decades of civil turmoil, and building non-existent political, economic and social structures (2010). NATO/ISAF forces should work in partnership with Afghan security forces to combat insurgent elements that terrorize the population and challenge the government. Insurgent forces continue to pursue a strategy of terrorist attacks, relying largely on suicide bombings (US Department of State 2010). Outlying provinces of Afghanistan are very inaccessible due to very few roads that are typically in poor condition; undependable cell phone signals, and none of the vital substantial communications established in

Kabul or the larger cities. Communicating their difficulties to the outside world is almost impossible.

I would like to see the following changes in US foreign policy towards Afghanistan based on the research provided above: the one trillion dollars in mineral deposits should be available to help Afghanistan get proper help, if the money is used in a proper way. As history has revealed some important topics, noted public policymakers have only focused on issues that would benefit their own interests and profit. These are some of the changes I would like to see, US foreign policy should put increased emphasis on education in Afghanistan and build more schools to educate girls and boys. The US diplomats should make more frequently visits to Afghanistan, in order to improve partnerships with government officials of Afghanistan. The US should research the possibility of an alternative product to the poppy, which has been a scourge on Afghan life, but which has been necessary for families to survive. Studies of soil conditions, climate, etc will help to facilitate solutions. All these are vital for Afghan people to see change, and it will make Afghan people safe and happy.

Summary

I would like to see the following changes in US foreign policy towards Afghanistan based research provide it above: In addition, the one trillion dollars in mineral deposits should be able to help Afghanistan get proper help, if the money is used in a proper way. As history has revealed some important topics previously noted, public policymakers have only focused on issues that would benefit their own interests and profit. These are some of the changes I would like to see, US foreign policy should put increased and emphasis on education in Afghanistan, and built more schools for girls and boys to study and get educated.

The US diplomats should make more, frequent visits to Afghanistan, in order to improve partnerships with government officials of Afghanistan. The US should research the possibility of an alternative product to the poppy which has been a scourge on Afghan life, but which has been necessary for families to survive. Studies of soil conditions, climate, etc will help to facilities this problem. All these are very vital for Afghan people to see change, and it will make Afghan people safe and happy.

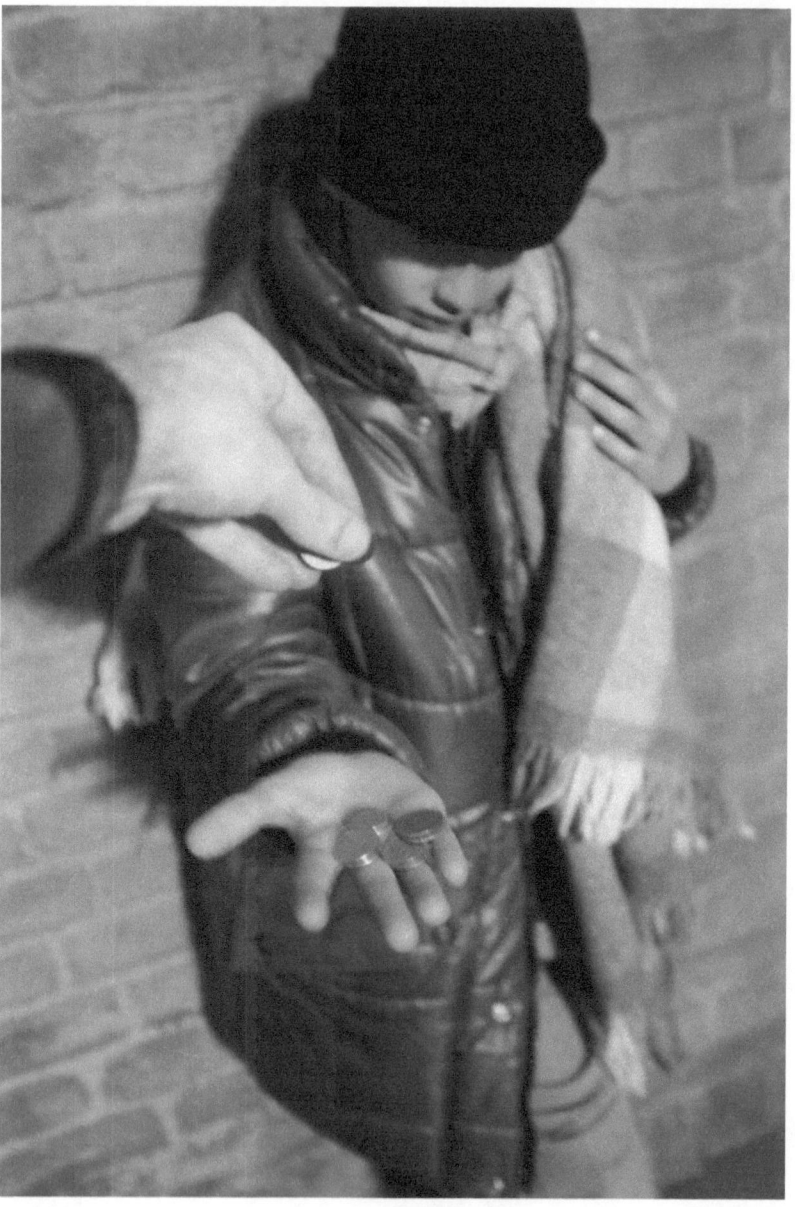

My Goals

My goal is to find a proper answer for my topic, using journals, books, editorials, the media, and more. There will be a lot of information to examine and to write about in this paper. The main reason for this paper is to get help for all Afghans who have been suffering during this ongoing war. In addition, I hope to aid in getting assistance from the US government. This study will be very demanding and time consuming, however, I am quite sure once the US puts complete attention to Afghanistan, things will get better, and will most definitely change. Most importantly, I will educate them, with this book. I will help them to get the proper aid through international government.

It will be very challenging for me to get them proper help, but I am sure that once this paper is finished and it gets to the right department and right people... someone in the international community will hear our voices and help our country rebuild and cease this ongoing war.

Challenges of my study

This study of public administration within Afghanistan was very demanding as there were not enough books and articles, or other previous research on this topic. It can take days, nights, and weeks, to find any information about Afghanistan public administration. As with most studies, my example may have biases, which would then take away from the accuracy of my findings. It creates a situation where one would ideally look around and talk to some people who are in highest authority to help Afghanistan.

I want to help them scream as loud as I can to get them the proper help. I hope future research will bring much needed assistance to Afghanistan from the United States in public policy.

REFERENCES

Augustan, C. (2004, April1). Retrieve February 1, 2010 from the international Monetary Fund:

http://www.imf.org/external/np/dm/2004/033104.htm

Colonel, D. (2006, March 16). Retrieve February 7, 2010 from USAWC STRATEGY RESEARCH PROJECT United States Army:

http://www.dtic.mil/cgi-bin/GetTRDoc?
AD=ADA448658&Location=U2&doc=
GetTRDoc.pdf

Clement, F. (2003). Retrieve March 7,
2010 from Conflict in Afghanistan:

http://books.google.com/books?id=bv
4hzxpo424C&pg=PA202&lpg=PA202
&dq =what+does+Parcham+means%
3F&source=bl&ots=bC0_vBny7E&sig
=BrsEgdQ5ZSVgwhAku0Hie23v6YM
&hl=en&ei=P_aaS5rgFsP68Abtjun9D
Q&sa=X&oi=book_result&ct=result&r
esnum=10&ved=0CBwQ6AEwCQ#v=
onepage&q=&f=false

Greg, S. (2010, February 16). Retrieve February 17, 2010, US strategy in Afghanistan deserves more than lip service.

http://www.theaustralian.com.au/news/opinion/us-strategy-in-afghanistan-deserves-more-than-lip-service/story-e6frg6zo-1225832357380

Gasper, P. (2001, December) Retrieve March 6, 2010, International Socialist Review: Afghanistan, the CIA, bin Laden, and the Taliban:

http://sif.org.ohio-state.edu/Gasper.pdf

Josh, R. (2009, October 26). Retrieve February 4, 2010, from LEW: No surge of civilians in Afghanistan after review:

http://thecable.foreignpolicy.com/ posts/2009/10/26/lew_no_surge_of_ civilians_in_afghanstan_after_review

Kenneth, K (2006, April2). Retrieve March 6, 2010 from CRS report for congress: Elections Constitution and Government:

http://pards.org/crs_country/CRSRepo rtAfghanistanElectionsConstitutionAn dGovernment(November2,2006).pdf.

Lister, S. (2006, September 1). Retrieve February January 25, 2010, from Afghanistan research and evaluation unit: https://wikis.uit. tufts.edu/confluence/display/FIC/ Afghanistan+Publications

Najumi, N. (2002) Retrieve March 6, 2010, from the book of rise of Taliban in Afghanistan: mass mobilization, civil war:

http://books.google.com/books?hl=en &lr=&id=wR4qmiOAvUC&oi=fnd&pg= PR5&dq=what+region+was+Afghanist an+before+democracy&ots=VF2gq6Y vqS&sig=Rdk7X4XNANumKy3dzOX

kg06FJdc#v=onepage&q=before%20
democray&f=false

World Bank: (2004, April 1). Retrieve
February 9, 2010, from Afghanistan
Research and Evaluation Unit, and
the Poverty Reduction and Economic
Management Sector Unit South Asia
Region:

http://wwwwds.worldbank.org/servlet/
WDSContentServer/WDSP/IB/2004/
04/28/000012009_20040428100221/
Rendered/PDF/284350AF.pdf

Blake, H. (2010, June). Say what?
Afghanistan has $1 trillion in untapped
mineral resources? Retrieved June

18, 2010 http://blog.foreignpolicy. com/posts/2010/06/14/say_what_ afghanistan_has_1_trillion_in_ untapped_mineral_resources

Cordesman, A. (20097, October). US Strategy in Afghanistan Drugs and Insecurity in Afghanistan: Retrieved June 18, 2010 No Quick Fix http:// csis.org/publication/us-strategy-afghanistan

Costa, A. (2008, January). Third International GLOBSEC Conference: Retrieved June 18, 2010 http://www. unodc.org/unodc/en/about-unodc/ speeches/2008-01-17.html

Katzman, K. (2010, June). Afghanistan: Post-Taliban Governance, Security, and U.S. Policy Retrieved July 10, 2010. http://www.fas.org/sgp/crs/row/RL30588.pdf

SAARC Nation: Afghanistan journey to the land of Afghanistan Retrieved June 18, 2010 http://afghanistan.saarctourism.org/history.html

US Department of States: (2010, February). Afghanistan Country Specific Information: Retrieved June 18, 2010 http://travel.state.gov/travel/cis_pa_tw/cis/cis_1056.html